The History of Wine in Africa and Asia

-Includes African, Persian, and Indian Wines, and Chinese, Russian, and Turkish Wines-

by

Edward Randolph Emerson

British Library Cataloguing-in-Publication Data
A catalogue record for this book is available from
the British Library

Contents

AFRICAN, PERSIAN, AND INDIAN WINES

A REGION that was thought at one time likely to be a strong rival to France's supremacy in viticulture, but which, largely on account of the stubbornness of the people most interested, has "Cape proven only a moderate success, is the wines." region in the south of Africa known as the Cape of Good Hope. Its wines are known and spoken of as " Cape wines," and at one time immense quantities of them were sold in England. Since the Cape belonged to England, England of course made the laws, and through mistaken notions made the duty into England very low. This had its natural effect, and made quantity and not quality the object of every vineyardist. It also acted against the wines, for they were mainly used in England for blending purposes, and although very cheap, yet the people as a whole seldom had a chance to purchase them in their original state. The vine was first brought to the Cape in 1650 by the Dutch,—at least so the Dutch say; there are others, however, who ascribe its introduction and cultivation to the French, when, after the revocation of the Edict of Nantes, the Dutch settled a colony of French emigrants at a place called Franschehoek. It is true that the French did settle there, but when one observes the utter carelessness and the absolute disregard for situation and facilities shown in the selection of sites for the location of the vineyards, there can be little doubt but that the assertions made by the Dutch that they were the first to plant vineyards is true; for no Frenchman with the least knowledge of viticulture would be guilty of such foolhardiness. Soil that would prove of great value to the cultivator is neglected, and other soil that is difficult of manipulation, hard of access, and in every way inferior is chosen and cultivated; and no amount of argument or persuasion could induce the Boer to change, after he had once made up his mind that his selection was the best. Precedent in the Dutch mind is something to be revered, and "the wis-_{Boer reverence for precedent.}dom of their ancestors" is almost infallible. It differs from the precedent of the Latin races in this respect: while the Latin has a great regard for it, it is more from downright laziness, but to the Dutch precedent is pure veneration, to be followed from generation to generation.

The casks used for the storage of wine in the cellars of the Cape merchants were not only things of use but were, and are, things of beauty. Made to contain seven or eight hundred gallons, their outer surfaces are so finely polished that they almost reflect one's face. Brass instead of iron is used for hoops, and the chimes or ends are also covered with the same material. The heads of the casks are very often handsomely carved in allegorical and historical figures. The bungholes are covered with heavy plates of brass, so fastened that they can be securely locked; the faucets are made of brass, and were meant to be opened with a key. Every day these casks had to receive attention, for to keep them in their proper condition required that dirt of no kind should come in contact with them. So large were the cellars, and so wealthy were the merchants, that the possession of a hundred or more of these casks was very common indeed.

But if care and attention is bestowed upon the casks, it is the reverse with the wine. The cultivation is thoroughly haphazard and careless; wines

that nature intended should be excellent and bene-
ficial to mankind are horrible and a detriment to the
users of them. Ofttimes the grapes are allowed
to ripen lying on the ground, no atten- Carelessness
tion whatever being given to them; taken in wine-
making.
when they are ready for the press, — ripe
grapes, green grapes, decayed grapes, vine leaves,
soil, twigs, and anything whatever, — all are treated
alike, and all are pressed together. A large quantity of bad wine is all that is required or desired.
To ameliorate this condition is almost an impossi-
bility; it has been tried time and again, but without
enough success to warrant its continuance. No
care is given even to the training of the vine, and
the materials used for its fertilization are of the
commonest and worst possible kind. The pressing
season is never given a thought, so far as the condition of the grape at the time is concerned. When
the month or week arrives that the grandsire first
pressed his grapes, then grapes must be pressed, be
they ready or not. Fermentation is allowed to
have its own way, and nothing is ever done to inter-
fere with it; in fact, the art of cider-making is elaborate when compared to the methods used by the
Cape people when making their wine. They have
one practice that to an outsider may seem strange,

and it might also influence, adversely, the mind of a prospective purchaser if he should happen to be nigh when it is done. While the wine is fermenting, large pieces of freshly killed meat are suspended in it for several days at a time. It is said to greatly improve the meat: the wine is to be sold. They also add great quantities of Capesmoke, a species of brandy that is made from the refuse of the winepress, and anything else that will ferment, and is so execrable that even the Boers refuse to drink it. The Hottentots and Kaffirs are said to be very fond of it, and the innocent Boer sells them large quantities. There are good wines produced at the Cape, but such is the reputation of the wine as a whole, that the good suffers in consequence, and the standard is placed very low.

The prohibition of the Koran has done very much toward the abolishment of viticulture in the northern part of Africa. Years ago Egypt was celebrated for her Mareotic wine, but when the followers of Mohammed took possession and overran the whole of North Africa, interest in vineyards for the purpose of wine-making soon ceased. The Mohammedan religion is very explicit in its condemnation of this species of cultivation, and the necessity of having the vineyards in the hands of one of a different faith opened fields for blackmail that the follower of Allah had no desire to submit to. So he quietly purchased his wine, and very quietly drank it. One trick attributed to the Mohammedan is the boiling of his wine; this removes the objections made in the Koran, as it is the fermented juice of the grape which is forbidden. Elephantiasis, or the swelling of the legs, is a good excuse for the use of wines; it is claimed that wine drinkers are never affected with it, and it is a fact that the Mohammedans are common subjects, while the Jew is exempt.

In Algiers grapes are grown of very superior quality, from which wine is made that is said to be superior to the best Hermitage of France. Around Tunis is made a variety of white wine that is remarkable for its keeping qualities and small percentage of alcohol. To improve this defect, for it must be so considered in their estimation, the natives add quicklime to it! Morocco produces a wine that greatly resembles sherry, and by some experts it is pronounced better. But the great drawback to viticulture in these North African countries is the frequent visits of the locust, which, in a few hours may entirely destroy the labor of years, and as there has been no known remedy, the

The Story of the Vine

raising of grapes is considered too hazardous and risky an undertaking, except in a very small way.

If to Persia we cannot ascribe the birthplace of the vine, we must at least call it the nursery, for

Persia the nursery of wine-making. to Persia the ancients with one accord ascribe their first knowledge of the vine and wine-making. The wines that are made in this country to-day rank very high in the favor of experts, and could the Persians be induced to use more modern methods in their vinification it is thought by many that her wines would lead the world. His religion, however, is an obstacle that will keep him back, and while the Persian makes fine wine, he cannot or will not make it in sufficient quantities to materially affect the market. The Persians in many respects are more liberal in their belief, and refuse in numerous ways to obey the

Wine vs. the Koran. precepts of the Koran; perhaps it would be better to say that they are more adept in dodging the question, for they openly use wine whenever they think it is necessary. Some, of course, are more strict than others, but there are many incidents that show how even these faithful followers of the Faithful will occasionally yield to temptation, and even let others see their fall from grace. An instance of this kind is told of an old

African, Persian, and Indian Wines

Mussulman who had been employed for a great number of years by an English gentleman. Being on the point of death he was ordered a glass of wine by a European physician, which he at first refused, observing, " I cannot take it, it is forbidden in the Koran." After a few minutes' pause he turned to the doctor, saying, as he raised himself on his bed, " Although it is forbidden, give the wine; for it is written in the same volume, that all you unbelievers will be excluded from paradise; and the experience of many years has taught me to prefer your society in the other world, to any place to which I could be advanced with my own countrymen."

Many of the Shahs were openly addicted to the use of wine, and not a few of them were very fastidious in their taste. Golden goblets and golden flagons were very often used at their feasts. " It is written that Shah Husseyn, son and successor of Soliman, published an edict prohibiting the use of wine, as forbidden by the Koran, and ordered all wine vessels in his own cellars to be publicly staved in, and forbade the Armenians to bring any more under a heavy penalty. This gave great alarm to the grandees and eunuchs of the palace, in consequence of which they applied to the King's grandmother, who was herself a lover of wine. Resolved

The Story of the Vine

to conquer the monarch's scruples, she feigned sickness. The physicians prescribed wine, but this she refused to take unless the Shah himself, who had presented it to her, should first drink of it. This he was unwilling to do, through religious motives, but these she overcame by quoting the Persian maxim that kings are subject to no law, and whatever they do, they commit no sin. By this artifice the prince was ensnared; he drank a large cup of the wine, which he liked so well that he was scarcely ever sober afterwards."

It frequently happens, even in this land of cheap labor, that it does not pay to gather the fruit, the **Persian grapes.** vines bear to such an extent, and it is left to rot upon the vine. The clusters, too, are exceedingly large and perfect, but the grape itself is what causes wonder to those who see it for the first time. It is seldom smaller than a good-size damson plum, and is ofttimes larger; one in fact is a fair mouthful. The taste and flavor far surpass anything in the grape line in any other country on the globe.

When the outlook is good for an increase in prices, the Persian vineyardist has a simple method of keeping his grapes in perfect condition; it consists of putting a linen bag over each cluster, and allowing it to remain on the vine until the next spring, or until such a time as he thinks advisable.

Wine is never sold by the measure in Persia, weight being the method used in determining the quantity desired. The prices differ, however, and in the end it amounts to the same thing, only it does seem a little odd to think of buying twenty-five pounds of sherry, ten pounds of port, and a hundred pounds of claret. The Persian vineyardist is very particular in storing his wine, and pays great attention to the construction of his cellars, and to their cleanliness. Coolness is the one object sought, and to acquire this a stream is often so deflected that a part of it, at least, will flow through the cellars and cool the air. Many of the cellars are provided with seats, so that the wine can better be enjoyed. Instead of barrels, jars of clay and large flasks made of glass are used for storing purposes.

Another feature of the wine business as carried on in Persia—one that causes the traveller to wonder—is the custom of putting only ten bottles in a case, instead of twelve, as we do. It is only fair to say that ten bottles are enough; each bottle, or *carabas* as they call it, holds about thirty quarts. Ten such cases as these, even if there be only ten bottles to the case, should be a year's supply for any man who considers himself a moderate drinker.

The principal wine-growing district of Persia is Shiraz, and the wines from this region are thought

Shiraz. to be essential to happiness, according to an old proverb which says, " Who will live merrily should take his wine from Shiraz, his bread from Yesdecast, and a rosy wife from Yest." Although the greater part of the wine which Persia produces is consumed at home, large quantities of it are exported to Hindostan, China, and Japan; some to England. The vineyards of course are never tilled by the Persians themselves, on account of their religion, but by Armenians, Guebers, or Jews, who are licensed and taxed very heavily for

Intoxication. the privilege. When intoxication is desired, the Persian very often mixes with his wine an extract of hemp, which has the faculty of making a little wine exceedingly inebriating; seemingly the effect is the same as produced by brandy or whiskey, the difference lying in its action. The user or drinker, though intoxicated, is seldom if ever quarrelsome. The Persians have a saying that "if Mohammed had been sensible of the pleasures of Shiraz, he would have begged God to make him immortal there," and although the faithful often

African, Persian, and Indian Wines

boil their wine, they manage in many ways to enjoy it in its natural state, and still be faithful.

It is not generally known that India produces wine, nevertheless she does, and many of her wines, both white and red, are of excellent quality, commanding fair prices. A The wines of India. variety made in the northern part of India is remarkable for its alcoholic strength; so strong is it that two small glasses, it is said, will intoxicate the average man. Like the Persian, the East Indian is hampered a great deal in his liking for wine by his religion, but, like his fellow-religionist, he seems to indulge his appetite or craving whenever he is so inclined. Before the advent of Mohammedanism, the Hindoo was of a very convivial nature, and wine-drinking and wine-making were practised on a large scale. Bacchus, in fact, was said to have been born in India; the story of Bala Rama compares so closely to the Roman and Grecian myth The Hindoo Bacchus. of the God of Wine that the story of Bacchus could easily have been woven from it. The Goddess of Wine among the Hindoos is Sura-dévi, and she still holds her position, and is revered by all. The Indians claim that it was Bacchus who taught them the art of pressing grapes and making wine, and that he resided in his capital of Nysa, in the modern Punjaub. He ruled India so well that after his death he was adored as a god.

In Golconda upon the hills the vine flourished luxuriantly, and wine was made in plenty, but for a long time its cultivation was forbidden, and what wine was used was drunk in secret. The story of how at last foreigners were allowed to plant vineyards and make wine is very neat, and shows a little piece of duplicity on both sides. It is related that the great Akbar was in much need of good gunners, **Legend of the foreigner who must have wine.** and by offers of large salary and rewards induced a number of sailors from various English vessels that were trading in his dominion to enlist in his service. One of these, a man who must have had an eye to the future more than to the present, was selected and told to fire at a carpet which Akbar had had suspended for a target. The test was a very easy one, but the fellow deliberately missed it. He was reproved and among the other names that were hurled at him was impostor. In no wise disconcerted, yet with an air of pretended humility, the fellow answered that his sight was bad, from having been debarred from the use of wine for such a long period, and he added that if he could but have one good drink of wine, he would hit a much smaller carpet at a greater dis-

tance. After considerable discussion as to where
the wine was to be procured, King Akbar, in order
to discover whether the man could do as he claimed,
gave the order for some wine to be brought, and in
some mysterious way a cupful, a little more than a
quart, was found and given him. This he drank,
and then, seemingly without taking aim, fired at the
smaller carpet and hit it square in the centre.
Every one present applauded him, and Akbar
ordered it to be recorded that " wine was as necessary to Europeans as water to a fish, and to deprive
them of it was to rob them of the greatest comfort
of their lives," and he then and there gave permis-
sion for foreigners to plant and cultivate vineyards
in his dominion.

From the island of Ceylon comes another story of
the same nature, and so alike are the two in sub-
stance that they are doubtless sprung A Cingalese
from some common source; but the tale is tradition.
good and will bear repeating in conjunction with
the above. At the time the island was first visited
by the Dutch, the Cingalese were a very temperate
people, and although wine was used it was considered a heinous offence, and great was the aston-
ishment of the natives at the fondness shown for
wine by the Christians. The quantity used was to

The Story of the Vine

their minds appalling, even cause for resentment, until they considered it almost an insult for a Christian to drink in their presence. The King of Candy had become greatly attached to a certain Dutch merchant, who settled on the island and had in more ways than one been of great benefit to him. Aside from the mercenary side to the acquaintance, there was a feeling of strong friendship, on the part of the King at least, and he was often in the habit of chiding the Dutchman for his wine-drinking propensity. On one occasion having called his friend to his presence, he exclaimed, " Why do you thus disorder yourself — so that when I send for you on business, you are not in a capacity to serve me ? " But Hans was not altogether overpowered by his libations, and what is more to the point, he had by this time become somewhat tired of this constant chiding, and he resolved that now was the time to put a stop to it once for all. So without further excuse he told the King "that as soon as his mother had deprived him of her milk, she supplied the want of it with wine, and that ever after he had accustomed himself to it." Hans had struck aright, and ever afterwards he was allowed to enjoy his wine without complaint, but his reply gave rise to the adage, "Wine is as natural to white men as milk to children."

African, Persian, and Indian Wines

The East Indian viniculturist very often employs a method of stretching out his wine that in this country would be an utter failure; but there, owing to the difference in climate, the use of boiling water and a little yeast poured on the lees, or refuse of the press after the first pressing, makes a very agreeable and pleasant tasting drink, and one that can be sold very cheaply; this, in a land so thickly populated, and so subject to famine as India, must indeed be a boon to the masses.

A very cheap wine.

There is a certain something about pure wine that is almost indispensable in such a climate, and medical research proves that he who will use it judiciously is benefited above those who refrain from its use. The Hindoos realize this fact, but religious scruples make hypocrites of them, and debar them from the open enjoyment of wine to a great extent. From the earliest installation of Mohammedanism, however, revolt against this precept of Mohammed was quickly instituted, both by the powers and the people. The clergy itself often connived at its use, and in many respects aided the " power that be " to conceal from his intimates the fact of his drinking the forbidden juice of the grape.

Mohammedan hypocrisy.

s

The Story of the Vine

The following incident will impart a faint idea as to the extent of this duplicity. A certain King A commander of Oude, known and admired for his of the faithful who justice as well as for the fatherly care he would drink. manifested for his people, showed a fondness for wine. How he acquired this fondness history fails to tell, whether from a sly drink now and then, or just by hearsay, we are left to judge for ourselves; but after acquiring the taste, he was anxious, as an upright son of the church, to maintain the appearance of being a good and true believer. For a long time he was in a quandary; he valued his wine and he also valued the reputation he had established for holiness, and he found it very difficult to make the two harmonize. The idea that he could dispense with one and retain the other was absurd: he wanted both and both he determined to have. There was but one person he could trust, yet he did not know how to accomplish his desire even should he confide in this man, an old trusted servant whose only duty was to attend to the hookah-burdar. At length he consulted a pious and learned mufti whose regard for monarchical favor was as strong as the odor of sanctity with which he gratified the spiritual longings of the faithful. The mufti understood the case in all its bearings, as any true believer would not fail to do, but what puzzled him was how to advise in order to keep the matter secret. Many plans were thought of and discussed, only to be rejected on one score or another. Some because they were too elaborate and difficult of accomplishment, and others because they were too easily detected. Suddenly the King bethought himself to call his old servant into the conference, and listen to what he had to suggest. The old fellow, after hearing the case, thought for a little while, and proposed that the wine should be placed in lieu of water in his hookah bottom. "Excellent! excellent" said the mufti, "that can bring no scandal on our faith." He took his leave of the King, but he soon found occasion to return and ask a favor, which, as he was in the secret of the hookah, the King could not do otherwise than grant. In the meanwhile, the King enjoyed his wine in perfect security, and was considered one of the most faithful of the prophet's disciples. Thus was the church benefited, and at the same time the King had at his command a ready and handy means of supplying himself with wine whenever he desired it.

CHINESE, RUSSIAN, AND TURKISH WINES

THE followers of Confucius have not the same religious scruples against the use of wine as their more southern neighbors, the Hindoos. Frugality has more to do with the sobriety of the *Sobriety due* Chinese than laws, although in a large *to frugality.* part of China it is thought to be a sin to cultivate fruit for its juice alone, whilst the ground that its growth would occupy could produce sustenance for many individuals, who might otherwise perish from hunger. The vine, however, is cultivated extensively in many parts of China, and wine is often made, that according to the tales of different travellers is of excellent quality. To be able to drink of it one must be where it is grown, for none of it ever leaves the country. In China the outside world, as we all know, is never considered, and for this reason many are not aware that the Chinese are rare judges of wine. Wine-making, as with gun-powder and other inventions, according to the Chinese, was first discovered in China, and their account of the discovery and its effect is very plausible.

The story goes that wine was first made by an ingenious agriculturist named I-tye during the reign of the Emperor Yu, or Ta-Yu, in the year 2207 before Christ, and that as the con- *A Chinese legend of the first wine.* sumption of it was likely to be attended with evil consequences, the Emperor explicitly forbade its use, and expressly interdicted its manufacture. He even went so far as to renounce it himself, and dismissed his cup-bearers, lest, as he said, the princes his successors might suffer their hearts to be effeminated with so delicious a beverage. But even in 2207 B.C. the framing of laws was one thing, and their enforcement decidedly another. The people had tasted of wine and, law or no law, were going to taste of it again.

Doctor Hales in his *Analysis of Chronology* supports the conjecture that I-tye was a near descendant of Noah's and it was from Shem's family he acquired his knowledge of viticulture and vinification. The writers of the *Universal History* allege " that Noah himself, being discontented with the party that had been formed to build the tower of Babel, separated from the main body, and with some followers, travelling eastward, at last entered China and laid the foundation of the empire." If either of the above be correct, the contention of the Chinese that they first discovered wine is remarkably well founded.

In 1836 B.C. we have another account of how the Emperor Kya,—by some called the Nero of China, A legendary — in order to gratify a whim and also to wine-bath. make a spectacular appeal to his people, had prepared an immense reservoir which he had filled with wine of the choicest kind, and ordered some three thousand of his subjects to jump into it and disport themselves as they pleased. Undoubtedly this is the first mention of a wine-bath in history, and the credit must be given to the Chinese for its discovery. The Chinese, like the ancient Romans, carried the use of wine to an excess, and spent thousands of dollars to gratify their vanity. It is told of the Emperor Kèè that, in order to indulge his propensities for drinking, and also to please a favorite mistress, he built a room coated with jasper, had the furniture adorned with precious stones, and constructed ponds of wine in his palace.

Chinese, Russian, and Turkish Wines

The vine has undergone many revolutions in China. Every new emperor had something to say about its use. While many of them upheld its cultivation, and encouraged the people in partaking of its juice, some few of them were opposed to it, and did what they could to suppress it. When orders were issued for rooting up all trees that encumbered the grounds destined for agriculture, the vine suffered in common with the others, and so complete was its extirpation during certain reigns that even its memory was forgotten in some provinces. This practice of extermination has led several historians into the error of ascribing the use and making of wines to a very modern date, for when the edict was cancelled against the cultivation of the vine, the people had to look to an outside source for their plants, and virtually had to begin again from the starting-point.

Extermination of the vine.

Wine has always been a drink of honor, and was used by cities and municipalities as presents to their viceroys and governors. In 1373 A.D. the Emperor Tay-Tsu, who had ascended the throne several years before, accepted some wine from the city of Tai-yuen for the last time with this remark: " I drink little wine, and I am unwilling that what I do drink should occasion any burden

A drink of honor.

The Story of the Vine

to my people." From 140 B.C. to the fifteenth century the vine can be traced without a break, but after that time there are several intermissions, which confuse the historian in his researches. There are numerous records of vines being brought from foreign countries, but no record of their subsequent cultivation or use. The use of wine in China at various feasts and celebrations is very important, and all invitations mention the fact. The following copy of a wedding invitation will give the reader an idea of its importance. " To the great head of study: On the 8th day of the present moon, your youngest brother is to be married. On the 9th having cleansed the cups, on the 10th he will pour out wine, on which day he will presume to draw to his lonely abode the carriage of his friend. With him he will enjoy the pleasures of conversation, and receive from him instructions for the well regulation of the feast. To this he solicits the brilliant presence of his elder brother; and the elevation to which the influence of his glory will assist him to rise, who can conceive ? " On the face of it a flattering and kind invitation, but woe betide the receiver if he attends the feast upon the strength of receiving it. The guests that are expected to attend receive at least three, more often four or five, of these missives, all couched in the same flowery style. On the day previous to the feast, another style of solicitation is sent on rose-colored paper, and on the day appointed an invitation is sent notifying the guest that all is ready, and nothing lacking except himself. When all are assembled and have partaken of some light refreshment, the dinner commences; the wine cups are filled, the host arises, and every guest follows his example, each holding a cup in both hands; after saluting each other they drink the contents, and then sit down to the repast. Wine is drunk on the serving of every course, and often on the appearance of every new dish.

Wine at a Chinese dinner.

The practice of pledging each other at a banquet is as common in China as in America, but the ceremony is slightly different. With the cups held in both hands the guests move to the centre of the room, raising and lowering their cups—the polite way is to touch the ground—three, six, or nine times, watching each other strictly till their cups are brought to their lips at the same instant, when they drink the contents and, turning them downwards, show that not a drop has been left. The retreat is in the same ceremonious manner, all bowing and saluting before taking their seats. The arrangement of the guests at the tables is more comfortable than after our method, and the serving of the viands is unique and in the minds of some preferable to Occidental methods. Each guest has a table to himself, and is served by his own servants, whom he brought with him for the purpose. The Chinese never say grace before beginning a repast, but instead they have a rule which is rigidly adhered to on every occasion. The master of the house, when his guests are all assembled, takes a cup of wine and, after bowing to the company, solemnly advances to the courtyard, and raising his eyes and the cup to heaven pours the wine upon the ground, as an offering of respect and thankfulness unto the deity. On the day following the feast the host sends a large red paper to each of the guests apologizing for the inferiority of the dinner, especially the wine; an immediate reply is returned on the same kind of paper, and in the same flowery language, decrying the host for his belittlement of the feast, and praising it to the skies.

In Japan the climatic conditions are such that the vine is only grown as a curiosity, rather **No native Japanese wines.** than for profit. The fruit is never made into wine, but is salted, and a kind of salad is made that is quite pleasant to the taste.

Chinese, Russian, and Turkish Wines

The Japanese are great wine drinkers, but they are compelled to import all they use.

Only the southern part of Russia is agreeable to the vine, and although considerable territory is given over to its cultivation, and a large quantity of wine is made, it is not appre- **Wines of Russia unappreciated.** ciated at home or abroad. For some unexplained reason the Russians as a rule dislike their own wines, and will sooner pay a high price for imported wines that are decidedly inferior, than pay a less price and get something better of their own countrymen. The same condition exists in America, and no one can tell why. The average American is a person of more than ordinary ability and discernment in other walks of life, but his love for the bottle and the label is only equalled by his ignorance of the contents of said bottle. Impartial analysis by experts have shown the wines of Russia to be in many cases of superior quality, and noted wine connoisseurs have given them a high rating for their exquisite flavor and bouquet. Their keeping qualities are good, and were it not for the unseemly prejudice of the Russians themselves, more wines could and would be made. There are, it may be said, only four districts in which wine is produced in Russia, namely Besasrabia, with the adjacent provinces of Cherson and Podolia, the government of Taurida, including the Crimea, the valley of the Don, and the Caucasus. The vine is also grown to a limited extent on the banks of the Volga, near Astrakhan and Kisjlar, and somewhat in Turkestan.

The most advanced methods are used both in cultivation and vinification. The government main-

Advanced methods of vinification. tains several schools where viticulture in all its branches is taught, and experiments of every kind, be they costly or not, are carried on. An Austrian monk who had been doing missionary duty in Persia in the early part of the seventeenth century was the first person to try to cultivate the grape in Russia for the purpose of wine-making. His efforts were so successful that the attention of the Czar Ivan Vassilievitsh was attracted, and in the year 1613 he issued an ukase telling his people to plant vineyards. The crown itself had planted and maintained at its own expense one hundred and thirty-five different vineyards of various sizes, and twenty-one of these are still owned by the state. The balance are now principally in the possession of private individuals. Peter the Great was exceedingly fond of good wine, and he did everything he could to advance its cultivation within his domain. His fondness for the grapes was such that he had them sent to St. Petersburg, and the nobility following his lead, made the industry an important one, but the price to the consumer was necessarily high, since about thirty-six pounds, after being packed in red millet so as to stand transportation, would cost at the vineyard between three and four dollars. What they cost when delivered in St. Petersburg cannot be told, for there are no records mentioning the fact. The grapes were unusually large and sweet, and the clusters were noted for their size, of which it is said some were nearly two feet in length.

There is a kind of champagne made in Russia that is to some extent popular, and commands a ready sale and a fair price, but it is never heard of outside of that country, for the simple reason that no one but a Russian could stand its intolerable sweetness and biting taste, which is caused by potash being used in the dosage. A certain class of the Czar's subjects require a wine that is very intoxicating, and to accomplish this a wine is made in which is placed, at the time of fermentation, unripe heads of the poppy. It is highly intoxicating and extremely injurious, but nevertheless great quantities are made and sold every year.

Almost every variety of grape known is grown

The Story of the Vine

and cultivated in the vineyards of this region, and such are the conditions that the majority are fruitful to a profitable extent. Vines from America, and there are thousands of them, grow side by side with those from remote Asia and Africa.

A great deal of the wine that is used in Russia comes from Georgia, the land which Russia absorbed in 1802. The Iberians, however, are not so much advanced in their methods as are the Russians, and although they make wine in large quantities, it is due more to the fact that the grapes are thrust upon them, as it were, than to any exertion or desire on their part. The vine is almost indigenous to the soil, and is seldom cultivated. It flourishes in all its native luxuriance, and although wild it seems to revel in its existence, and year by year to yield more and more. All theories as to cultivation and attention are knocked on the head when the vine is studied in Georgia,—or, as it is perhaps better known, Russia Transcaucasia,—the land fancied by many to be the home of Adam and Eve; and for a truth, no more favored spot can be found on this round world of ours for the garden of Eden. The hand of man is never needed here to till the soil. The rank growth of the tropics is not to be found, nor yet the dwarfed and shrivelled specimens

The vine in Georgia.

29

of vegetation so common in the farther north. Here the vine is allowed to seek its own pleasure, and instead of retrogradation advancement is *The garden* the result. So prolific is it that millions *spot of earth.* of clusters are left to decay or to feed the birds every year, since they are not converted to any profitable use.

The wine that is made from these grapes ranks with the wines of France, and surpasses some of them. Could conditions and circumstances be altered, Georgia wines would find a ready market at any time, but private methods are in vogue, and there seems no way in which they can be changed. The people themselves are great drinkers of their own products, seven or eight bottles a day being thought little of, yet so pure is the wine that intoxication is rarely the result. The price at which it is made and sold, two or three cents a gallon, is a great inducement, and it is not surprising that the people refuse to drink water.

The *boordook*, the skin of a goat or buffalo, coated with naphtha on the hairy side, and then reversed, is the favored receptacle for *Receptacles* holding wine in any large quantity. Like *for wine.* the Spanish *odore*, it has its disadvantages, and one must acquire by long and disagreeable practice a taste for wine that has once been in a *boordook*. The old method of putting wine in earthen jars and then burying them is also in vogue. A story is told of a recent traveller who, after attending an entertainment given by one of the princes of Georgia, was requested to step to an outhouse which he was informed was a wine cellar; but to his surprise there was nothing visible except the four walls and roof. There was not the slightest indication of a cellar of any sort, let alone a wine cellar. Not even a cup or glass could be seen— everything was as bare as an empty box. After an interval of several minutes, four men appeared with spades and began to dig up a portion of the cellar bottom; when about two feet of earth had been removed, there were brought to sight two immense earthen jars, each fully as large as a hogshead. The wine was served in long-handled solid silver ladles, and each guest was expected to drink at least one ladleful. Even the peasants who attended as spectators were given copious libations, but instead of silver ladles, earthen jars holding about two quarts were filled and handed to each individual, and in numerous cases the jars were returned entirely emptied of their contents. The sight of seeing a hundred or more *boordooks* standing on pieces of wood like

Chinese, Russian, and Turkish Wines

living animals is one that strikes the stranger with surprise; then to see the dealer draw the rich, dark red wine from them is, to say the least, sinister and inauspicious. But familiarity soon breeds contempt, the stranger's repugnance soon disappears, and such sights are taken as a matter of course.

The Iberians, though of the Mohammedan faith, never, as a rule, resort to subterfuge in order to excuse the drinking of wine. In fact it is the reverse, for wine is sold and drunk in the open market at all times during the day. It is told of the Sardar of Erivan that he defended his partiality for wine by saying that " the Koran affirms that the faithful shall have wine in paradise, a wine delicious to the taste, but not intoxicating, from which he inferred that the Prophet only intended that wine should not be drunk to excess, since it is sinful to suppose that what is lawful in heaven, is unlawful on earth "; and as all his followers have the same belief, the precepts of the Prophet have but little effect.

Wine vs. the Koran again.

In Turkey wine has very little chance of success, and although the Turks are great drinkers, few vineyards are to be seen. Some wine is made in the Ottoman Empire by Armenians and Jews, but its disposal is fraught

The vine tabooed in Turkey.

6

The Story of the Vine

with so much difficulty, and the vineyardist is so hampered by the religious views of the community, that it proves very often a source of loss instead of profit.

Some of the Sultans have been very strict in their observation of religious rules, and have often used very harsh methods to suppress and restrict the use of wine. The Sultan Solyman I. was a vigorous enemy to wine, and some of his mandates to check the progress of this irregularity were rigorous in the extreme. His favorite practice was to have molten lead poured down the throats of those of his subjects who were unfortunate enough to be caught using wine. Solyman II., his son and successor, went to the other extreme, and allowed **Solyman "the drunkard."** his people to pursue their own pleasure to such an extent that his reign is noted in history for being one of unparalleled debauchery. He himself was even nicknamed *Mest*, or drunkard. It was he who said, " Let others put their trust in man, I throw myself into the arms of the Almighty, and resign myself to His immutable decrees. I think only of the pleasures of the day, and have no care for futurity."

The following story is told of one of the Sultans, who, being one day on a hunting excursion, strayed

Chinese, Russian, and Turkish Wines

from his attendants. Being pressed by hunger and thirst, he was obliged to repair to a peasant's hut to procure some refreshment. The poor man immediately brought to the Sultan some brown bread and a pot of milk. The Sultan asked him if he had nothing else to give him, upon which the peasant presented him with a jug of wine. After drinking a good draught, the Sultan inquired, "Do you know who I am?" The man answered that he did not.

"I would have you know, then," said the Sultan, "that I am one of the principal lords of the Sultan's court."

After he had taken another draught he put the same question as before to the man, who answered, "Have not I already told you that I know you not?" The Sultan returned, "I am a much greater person than I have made you believe."

Then he drank again and asked his host for the third time whether he did not know him, to which the other replied, "You may depend upon the truth of the answer I have already given you."

"I am, then," said he, "no less a personage than the Sultan, before whom all the world prostrate themselves."

The Story of the Vine

The peasant no sooner heard the words than he tremblingly carried away the pitcher, and would not suffer his guest to drink any more. The Sultan, surprised at such behavior, asked him why he removed the wine. The peasant replied, "Because I am afraid that if you take a fourth draught you will tell me that you are the Prophet Mohammed, and if by chance a fifth, the Almighty himself."

This gentle rebuke so pleased the Sultan that he could not forbear laughing, and being soon rejoined by his people, he ordered a purse of silver and a fine vest to be given to the poor man who had entertained him so hospitably. The peasant, in a transport of joy for the good fortune he had experienced, exclaimed, " I shall henceforth take you for what you pretend to be, even though you should make yourself three times more considerable than in this instance."

Herbelot, the well-known French writer, tells in his *Bibliotheque Orientale* that there were some Mussulmen who were so religious and strict in their moral code that they would never call wine by its proper name, for fear of giving offence to the Prophet, and travellers were often cautioned not to use wine in their rooms, lest the carpets or mats on which the Mussulman said his prayers should be polluted.

Busbequis tells of an old man at Constantinople who, whenever he drank wine, summoned his own soul to take refuge in some corner of his body, or to leave it altogether, to avoid participating in the crime or being pol- Overcoming religious scruples. luted by such indulgence. Covering the mustaches so that they may not be defiled is a very common practice; while the wrong labelling of the bottles or jars is a daily occurrence. Every trivial excuse that can be invented so as to circumvent the mandates of the Koran is used time and time again, so fond is the average Mussulman of his wine.

When the desire for wine has once seized a Mussulman, expense and trouble is of no consideration, but in all cases secrecy must be maintained. Small leather bottles are much used for this purpose; sometimes leather tubes, after being filled with wine, are twisted around the body, and in that way the wine is smuggled into the home, where, when the servants have departed, it is enjoyed. Even the seraglio is not free from wine, for the women themselves are as great lovers of the juice of the grape as the men; but extraordinary precautions must be observed by them, for death is the penalty if they are caught drinking. Bottles that have contained Rosolio, an Italian cordial, whose labels are intact, are much used for the purpose of smuggling wine to the ladies. The sale of wine, however, is open, and the government derives from it a large portion of its revenue. This is especially true of the " restricted cities " and has given rise to the Turkish saying, " The cities forbidden to infidels abound with forbidden things."

Dr. Madden, an eminent authority on Turkish affairs, tells a story of a fellow who was very successful as a doctor, though in this country he would rank as a quack. When asked by an old acquaintance how he could presume to become a physician, and expose his life should one of the faithful die because of his ignorance, he replied that he had sufficiently learned the art from observing a regular practitioner at his late master's house, and he had acquired a comprehensive knowledge of prescriptions by testing the one that had been given to his master. It was a simple wine punch, of which the doctor himself partook. This gave him a very high opinion of its efficacy, and induced him to try it on himself. The results were gratifying, and, moreover, it was pleasant to the taste. He learned the secret of its manufacture,

A Turkish physician.

and having a desire to work for himself he set out as a doctor. In all cases he used this one prescription, and so salutary was it that he soon acquired a very large practice, and was greatly honored as a man of vast knowledge and wonderful ability.